SUELO TIDE CEMENT

Respire, Christina Vega-Westhoff & George Life

SUELO TIDE CEMENT

CHRISTINA VEGA–WESTHOFF

WINNER OF THE NIGHTBOAT POETRY PRIZE

NIGHTBOAT BOOKS / NEW YORK

ISBN: 978-1-937658-80-9

Design and typesetting by HR Hegnauer
Text set in Bembo Standard
Cover art (detail): *Respire*, Christina Vega-Westhoff & George Life

Cataloging-in-publication data is available
from the Library of Congress

Distributed by University Press of New England
One Court Street
Lebanon, NH 03766
www.upne.com

Nightboat Books
New York
www.nightboat.org

1 . SUELO

19 . ON SUELO | SOIL

25 . TIDE

51 . CEMENT

79 . COMPOST/COMPOSED

83 . (END)NOTES

85 . ACKNOWLEDGMENTS

SUELO

/

then in terms of water AGAIN—the immediate
avoidance of what is known as worms
and then in terms of who might be an effective
helper / or communicator. Take do you
know / as in motion beginning / if in the midst
of luxurious hunger / the bodies then at the shore

[...]

if you tried, but failed, it
was expected (they said / in the
papers) and simply a part of it
as in _____ and then _____
   ?

//

& in pieces of settled landmass
it is in this way unexpected
division which creates earth
anew //

how if paternalism's
presence as in us and them and
what we bring as if we as
separate from what

If you were in need of forgotten memory
or to seek the place of displacement
refreshed, as in, the sailors we
cleaned. / Foretold or not, these were
the promisings / we beyond (collaboration)
(promises) (carrots) (we want)
// and though the scientist speaks of
what you want to know, you cannot hardly
listen // as the rocks were
additions from the time before the land
emerged / and then attached // and then
separated / by mar / shoreline receding /
but the human remains still uncovered
in the earth of ocean
         if the "facts" "create" "imagination"
//
deforested & replanted
here (in the tropics) in ten years
thick—a path in constant need
of maintenance—or redistribution—sprouts
eliminated, at most

30% of what was and never the same
diversity. / And what seems unspoken
of is what could be called the furthest
spoke. And then this oncoming
onslaught as in desesperación,
filthy wanderings. First or third or fourth
or transparency in business and—
the great fear of the oncoming exposure—
as in you find you want to read of the
lifting. / (It seems like a long time to
continue with abstractions.) / Have to
find then replenished nourishings. / (Dream of all
the people who would offer to be your lover.)
Nearly asleep. / The first layer
           //

        if in the house by the sea on the hilltop
        with open walls what reaches you
        are two competing reggae(ton)
        songs—the party boat of the other
        visitors. If in comparison.

How ma(n)y assumptions—prejudices—come from the
most simplest of. To say, but no, I—
once you followed the path of where they had
been (when the man had been alive)
and in this particular view/vista of rock of ocean
and height above, it is recalled, though
fluently imbibed with the dissimilarities.

> I am watching as a ghost
> exhaling over the other one
> and that notion of a breath in
> unison as all encompassing care/
> eternity

says the radio—it makes me nervous
says the real estate sign—
says Polo's Beach—mata mata
            (nothing on what we call development)
Video/Images: lava pools—Sunday bulla—stars
    at night—clay (hugs) if possible—
    trapeze (tree over path to lava?)

reseeding

That an instruction to place is
re-entry. As in leaving both the collapsible
tent and air mattress for necessities of
bladder expecting again the stars the same
as if it were the same time and place then
again. Dawn had come. First light against
the edge of ocean and hills. Even with sleep awake.
The very large tucán at the watercooler
announcing first its presence and not
immediately leaving. Why large.
Imagine the weight of that beak
and if / how it must dip again and
again. Place as imagination. What
do we later reconstruct in dream that is
as if more well known (?).

The exotification of rock then—would it
be a sensual elopement or a question of
returned sight. How far back if
time is imaginable as any other
(than) fairytale. It was the calm
thought today that seemed out of place. The
quiet really. An opportunity for something
other than. Did you read your name
appropriately? It is easy to misread.
The sweet smell as in plantain's addi(c)tion
may as well have been rice.
And how did more green than mentality
affect what arose among us?
"I have nothing but a knowledge of
infinitesimal bliss" "Do you trust
me"   In those moments—
no. If your hands could only
be more clean. And yet we didn't
create our own soap.

The one-way track dug in. If you attempted
not to walk in a way in which you would
fall, but fell anyway. The stick could
be used to point at rock as in on-
site lecture. You know when the
exercise is useful or trade efficient.
To have a little efficiency. The house as
one degree. Quotient, adding up the
little tics it seems Jonathan
tells me not to. But where is he
from and what can he mean. And
we—do we know.
A toucan will (n)ever be regular houseguest
in the root of memory. As it once
was is not desirable. Humans
have long affected soil—and its composition—
and remodeled earth. And now are we
only thinking micro—are we dividing
up too many tasks. So that where can
responsibility (eventually) (even). As in we
ready for eating/entirety.

Place / memory / lapse
    and indeed the little ingredients
the point here maybe is just what
    is noticed as as equivalent
    encompasses.

If the vision were then a
part of your innermost treeness
    as in part/all of the fight is (materialized)
    within
        As lost art(if)(act) husk /
        fibrous entities / a chair of sand
        then the experience of annihilation
written overlays /
        counting your big sensations

and if here or there
as in the biggest it just happened (ing)
    (send)

Perceived as such, the voice carries—
forth—the cut/cat or the music/culebra.
The agony—the night entering
much too early without moon
with cloudless design—with
duct tape in recreation-izing
recolonization—new / neozonation
I am reading the words you are reading
snacktime creation. The
riff resonates yet we don't know why
or when or fonetic remembrances.
Across from

In the tree—from a hug,
blue circular patches as in little
coral beds from above as in
snorkeling looking down. To maintain
balancing not detectable from the outside.
Veins as conch shell intestines. Brains of
any number of creatures. Now precarious
left ankle balance. As in childhood
and the journey that flew page by page
romantic notion of tree journaling.
Now a workout to sit here. The trapeze
rearranged. The zigzag of the
path as in snakework shadow
along the ruin's spine. Hugging moss.
Veins inside—appear clinging to mass.
Not quite a distillation. Inst(i)(a)llation.
Footsteps that patter from seaside.
To see living life—or at
least this speckling.

/

brief encounters with trapeze
spatial reorganization

Images/Video:
  - cracked mud
  - ocean . texture
  - compost [pit
  - purple flowers etc

~~

then as to the side awakened
the father's footsteps encased in
soil samples as though unforgotten
how these entries/entities—bodies, earth
work again and again to clean
you tried waking just because the
stars could be spread open like
a map to underground
could be explained as in awakened
vision(ing) we wor(l)dless cried out
along with the turning
oceanic how the line kept
unfolding long intestinal fungi
~~I am savoring this belly of earth~~
forced your life to change in deep
resonating tones toked thirst snail
                              shell
                    bemoaning

far or not so far
time or wood shadow teak
the sense of toothma(r)(s)k passages
in undulations traveling the body.
When explored, the earth upside down
could awaken nostalgia
on the bed spread back from wall
the feet trace the snail's persistent
passage
flush of sun // sunrise
golden peak this leaf's
de – compo – sition
sitio
deco   you took it
posi   truly as
tío   **//**   let's hold
posit   forth together
flush

she says it can reteach you time
the daily noticings of
little garden
languages feel at the border before
the line ever shifting
another says that anxiety and deep breath
cannot coexist in the same body
how much a part of things we are

the shell—throw it back
not because it will
be nostalgic for its home but because
how often do you remember something
forgotten. When there are no deep
words to sing, listen(ing).

& the night as in a night time dream
to be called to return again and again the same
project as in time
we were sleeping or awoken
the leaves also of yuca (boiled, veined, ya)
to be eaten and embroidered on top of
if what is most inspiring is the movement through
softly the space winding you
revolutions, the stories uncovered kindly
as in a communal power if agreed to
if in soundwaves carried but faster as in light
for then we are lost as soon as found
yes, it is true for the systems
for the findings as though the government
were different and how frequently
the pride as if one had worked for
distancing. Now the eyes closing.
Would it be the time. Would we be
so amazing and for how long. When.

What was said aloud
floated and fell in silence and when we
left, we left each one in silence
or near silence—everything is
easily erased. Like this house we
occupy where every room is exposed, open
air, where what we bring will be
removed.
If ephemeral as the woman said
in an untranslated accent, showing
us the wares that would soon
decompose themselves. Something we
offered together—What do
we give to you soil
even as I write this, someone
approaching or distancing, footsteps
over leaves, branches,
and other decomposing
materials
to look at de-compositing/
osition as ~~the mos~~ creation
without qualifiers

ON SUELO | SOIL

ON SUELO

Taken from a blue canvas notebook with lines,
these writings are as happenings during a shared
experience based, among other commonalities, on
communal soil/suelo. One week, eight days/nine,
living in an open air structure, sharing meals,
chores, changing space, sleeping tents, and a focus
which became defined through conceptions of time
altered as in daily noticing or not. The
scope of the microscopic simultaneously
not the same. These then are my soil samples.
Though I looked at soil, I did not look at
it through the microscope when the others did.
At times the space away from shared space.
Because our conscious shared experience had
most to do with compost, decreation
emphasized.

SOIL

1. Privacy of/as a notion of disgust and requirement work in public any yet little spaces in the open air. If the man was around too much or the woman wanted to share too many things or the man became a surrogate for codependence—the land here though immediately a sand pit, first layer, is it only leftover/remnants of construction—the neighbor's piles of sand blowing through the clean clothes and the lot of us as if cast into sleep, itchy throat, red eyes. The woman behind us is actually taking action—which indicates speaking. The dog passes by the playground, having snuck out with his friend, the two trotting quickly away from Gaital. But on the walk up the other cerro, how much red as in clay overlaying soil. And is understanding the difference between soil and clay like understanding the difference between a rock that migrating 70 million years ago and one that emerged hace 3 million years ago or that a true organic has to do with carbon. In this information age, how much is quietly (or loudly) misunderstood or in ignorance held. If the soil project were taken to other parts of the country, what would unite it? If compost were a shared concept where a small garden of your own

were already common. If the same set of workshops repeated. It could be done also. How many materials localized? How this playground structure holds itself together—a series of arms—one set as if giving support to the mountain. Like a barracks the house at the corner—a story and a half higher—so that its white touches the white of the clouds and not the green of the mountain's trees where the orchids are being restored. Replanted. To join that day (of magic).

SOIL 2.

In discreet horizons
The compilation that accumulates in layers

To lose the history of the(ir) place
The associations above, below, and to the sides

Tierra firme
Packed
Living

Loose or displaced or runaway

We were attempting to live in intricate intersections

With living organisms or ~~lifeless~~ decomposed minerals and rocks

Many decomposers

    To be of not nots

TIDE

of less necessity than in other places
abandoned, the canon ship
the sound some soft repetition
it was high tide and then low tide
and then in between tide, when
we came down the road
passing the river once more fully
connected and before then when less
and the estuary, the man with head
bowed between knees so softly noticing us
as to give us hardly a glance
if the friend had written full
exposition or I had answered
it is a difficult affair having knowing
tore/tone always on a computer different
if exhausted and brief or merely sharp-witted
the man took to his back in the ocean
the ocean approached

overhead from the dune the little
waterfalls of sand. here we are
miraculously at the intersection
where the men boat in to store
their wooden boats and engines at the estuary

we have designed a compass
for measuring past time

precious awakening.
lately as if a backlash against the
word—commissary—comisión, la preciosa
naturaleza, la preciosura de la
niñez o el exotique get away or
the bottledrum—or for us perhaps—
paper wrapped chocolate with the white
& green sticker.

images of a leaf's decay. here
one sprouting a hole. there a field already
bespeckled. the first hooded sweatshirt
fisherman right here passing by.

not breadbasket, but leather
and all things vaca & cowboy & the
colonial early years & nostalgia

last
voyage across the continent—the one written
by another imagined

nonsense. it is law now. (the man walks
back) / viernes—(playa)

as if some presidents safer than others
or all safer than one

The feedtime frenzy as soon
as grain hits grass or political t-shirt
(free) hits crowd-member's han—

the gurgling of little fingers come together
line of pelican-like meandering
half moon. crackle of dying palms
s(h)ifted perspective then—
too young
that a sense of safety would
lead back to questions—identity,
place, privilege. the guarded set
officially public. just far away
enough to be inconvenient
and if without the privacy at
least the silence
low tide prayer.
how the length requirement
that leads to expert-like assertions
and the division between local
native. born where?

to have fulfilled the day
quota or week or month or other unknown
quantity at which end indivisible

the estuary
protected, but its buffer zone yet replanted cattle
grazing the lots along the road for sale or rent the
cement block houses the modern day tropical manual

how the silhouette—ghastly pink
official vs unofficial
the plastering of
candidates
slogan being open sesame
savior toasted risen son.
stung across the face submerging
only to emerge.
perhaps
among us/hen's eggs/patio/notions of dreaming

George chased the birds today.
and then the way in which they were
moving grazing and we were walking was
the same. flying & landing. flying &
landing. and it became tedious.

 on either side of us then swarms. less
in front

touching what is a white seed
on the cloth/dish sponge
but then flies up to the curtain
moth

  desertification desert–ification
  desertify vacation

it would grow through cement, erupting it.
as in without a plan designed or stolen
and combination of stolen design and
bankrupt & stolen out from under and
never were titled and the specifics
enormity. As in sovereignty in one
hand and the other—
   and the body—
& in the mind—
even with the design this ever constant
fractioning. to have been important
because _____

   (identity)   . the novel did not stop to
call (to be translated).
the land did not stop to be confused
missionaries of soil neither
to also be encasing the large building
the cement. the how many seeds of

_____.

how many supply side swindled.

not a study then, but as if merely.
to be also in love, but tested, testing.
to be the body in a cancelation of
production.
& to solve the problem that is not so
sightly.
- restarted
- coming up a
- the man then jumping over
& wiping wash—to back
in the morning there was a lover's breath
that pulled us down here
& the flushing fields on the walk
which we could not beat, even at
our pace
the fishermen passing us twice—~~once~~ in
the truck & then in departing, pushing
the wooden boats past anchor
the rosebud appeared when we thought we
had missed it. little pomegranate
hearth—how if you don't see the
                    body

no, to live very comfortably the
way we do, only complaining
the homeland hasn't/hadn't
having found other ways
in silence but not, since ever present
& caustic daydream—the bleached
log creating window
the bed from which the tree sprouted
or the other way around
click then, and again
another momentary image of the past
seeking

the water is clear & you see how
long you can hold your leg up, to give
it a place to rest on, driftwood in
balancing base catcher, as in, will
not let this body slip through
and also that the pen only cost 15 cents
now understood. it was not so much
clear as clearer. when it felt
like your lover nudged you, but in
lifting your head you saw how far away
you could upon returning your
gaze see the clear but striped fish

over the waves two kites
that first seem too enormous fish
or whales

our intentions are different,
the cry goes/
the guilt continuing
as
implications of the wealth of
the world are again & again thrown
before you.
and again & again.
a scream/
a cry/
the sky being emptied

a cow conniving(?) to glance
at you while the rest run away.

under the seeming symbols that say this is
impossible to read through just a logical conclusion
to the end of a line,
in telling of vocabulary of (the old _____
commerce unknown and how the bank in its
naming redundant/
    to strike at the ancient memory of what
a peso was
captured that marking of
the old club union—that acts as continuance
marking point—and what will happen then
in ten years—five
if you could be said to be not here, not
in this country or any other, having no
definable home but in reference to
others who do—if in this as nonexistence
sheltering's betrayal

no matter how you look at the ocean it will
never be enough—this empty desire for more

your life could always be dissected through
the lens of colonialism/post or otherwise
& the degree of disruptions or continuities
—the world then in its diet
    degree of more consumption
to cast away you suspect language
the net that though handstitched
and not deep water, will drag the ocean floor—
you saw it—on the way to the
house that looked like Switzerland on fantasy
pills & must be to be here consummated
where in view of the white sand beaches of
the island, that trick of real estate
the boon in which taxation or never
held papers or suspicion of
at what now the value

being wheeled past the window for change
on the global sphere gentrification
one wave after the other before you
can turn around plunged back under
we had the history of the region
quite unalike but each day
added up, another neighbor at
the door—pollito going to the neighbors

it is like a piece of broken map
to be actually involved in the series of projects
of which written dia-namics
diabolical diagnostic in doing
dying in doses dust counter(ed)(ing)
cultured array of diplomacy
to stay or not to stay or for how long (shore)
(if the record keeping or the brokeraging of)

to sink the hip deeper
being the meaning of the verb
learned in the primary song instruction
man stroking the hip cheek

that the ocean's supply was not inexhaustible
to tell them, we always thought more would
come in

what is
pronounced in English on the signs in passing

is all about luxury

these exclusions of personhood
ever more dramatic when beyond local
& into global

the national media in hiding
along the protest lined road(ing)
(for kind promisings-less) contraseña

to not have answered though brought along
misspelling—mistaken—or misphrasing
misfiring as in the excuse release of
our missiles please—so to cover in
mistletoe, ice broken through in skating
or by sunshine springtime as though to
have 4 official seasons were to have
real seasons as though this
were a place unreal or very really
lacking in reality perception
to have one as official that is not this—
what if the bird again & again walked by—
stood with you or longer than you to look
at ocean
(what in the body would replicate
    this sand dollar formation?)

the blue as in plastic gem jewelry
but not having been touched
and touching back—first a gentle slap
the wrist only slightly enreddened
but then in preventing and in the
thrust of responding the whole leg
marked by what could only be deemed
to be tentacles yet on the sand
seemed the most pliable unthreaded
cloth—
for the cake of the little edoll, the incoming
tunas and re-representations of monarchy
so that the entering & exiting of her
most majestic opposing realms
and it is not to say or hear her
special day in timing repulsing
to have been unradicalized or deemed so
or in comparison yearning—what
did in saying envision—in visioning
the young nun as if alive

confessing the love's profession talked out of
or as in whole body lying beneath the table
enfolding

if the call could not speak envolumed
the illumined first bell ringing

or the shade enmeshing only
be as
on the bicycle also departing
with the gaze set in conquering
to measure, to measure again
the first sounds of music
from the cliffside or the boat in
passing
t-shirt overhead, neck & nearly eyes

while the rat disease is killing
and this year camping banned
& last year certain city's carnavales
banned for violence excess
if we are talking of sustainability
where does the water come from
last year the summer lasted until
May and this year still mid or early
mid-leaning, late if like before
how many houses will be going without
or buying
if today—a weekday—the beach
is remarkably cleaner
to say nothing of the city or the
burnings

then
as in
projects of reforesting
& buildings from (which) demolishings
    pour forth new edifices
    by nightly/mighty witchery
    say the potion
    is in the bottle
    in the cooked
    bottle, sand
    wet, but still legible
    & not in Your language
    what other container enclosing
    finally set
    come closing in on one part of
    _____ (place) at a time
    but everywhere the looming present
expectation of in(flux) (coming)
of (the) wealth(y)
who as in owners
    remain
    in-site (side)

it was easy to belong with everything
  in separate stances
    to catalogue the lions/
    tigers. crocodiles/alligators
    eels/snakes
    mamallenas/bread puddings
    chicheme/crab
    yogurt but no leche
      cheese but no green
        beans
      close as coffee
      & linaza
      seed formation
      vacas staring at you
        armadillo flattened
          anteater rotting
          pony tied to the tree
      next to its mother
        expat teenagers   out of
          range of chickens

well-intentioned but not yet responsible
the organization in the hand
or cradlefall donation
finding in the phrasebook another
line of no body says that here
collapsing from the weight of nothing
out of body
from the video & in perking
colliding
plate
tectonic
lava landscape
now limping from (through) sunrise
soaked petition
to no doctor begging
  forced—sand
      smuck
    line in which every horizon
  has been recognized
  up close
  zoom the person

Low tide   Mon (4:22 am)
                    4:48 pm
              Tues (5:30 am)
                    6:03 pm
             Wed (6:45 am)
                    7:14 pm, High = 1:14 pm
Mañana   Thurs (7:44 am)
   (departure) 8:16 pm

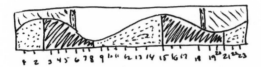

High 2:36 AM   10.7 ft   First Light 5:49 AM
Low 8:40 AM   0.1 ft   Sunrise 610 AM
High 3:00 PM   10.9 ft   Sunset 6:24 PM
Low 9:06 PM   -0.5 ft   Last Light 6:45 PM

as the shore expands
the shadow reaching more & more
what is ungraspable for maybe
an hour more
(between tide(s))
sun yet overhead
the kite, the sparrow,
the runner,
the reader of interviews
the swing set just back, in the grove
go beyond the ending
or back to it

"where's my sweet ambrosial
chocolate or batido de piña"

CEMENT

/ broken down, water contains
within it particles of earth

/ the sound recording of
        tree rings
    as though in motion with the
      needle going round

/ will it be privately owned or
      in the public domain

/ between molecules & spirit

on tin, expected/
in exchange breakdown astuteness
      in excess of liabilities
        tangible
    element responsible for
  /   density in
        sight

could not escape thought
could not breathe
as adequate
as dry parchment
as hopelessly joy bereaved
or in labeling
micro
been in the grasp
of (im)(un)balancing
the heart or the feather

& the tea of Dr Wang not
enough
in deprivation of
community or
in bereavement it's said
the ovaries shutting down
as orphan response
says the website
all the relatives
now approaching

if the farmers are always coming from
elsewhere

imagine the entire
family's lineage as in connection
most recent to place

cast as in held in
the hand as
the blackest soil in
the tropics and for sale

along with—

case enclosed
        setting
loss of water

& in fine breath
        attaining

then as part of envelopment
    body piled on top of hands
            on top of
            body

another dead ant
        sheet pulled back

& how that is yet
            —good sign, good sign

/ along the Pacific high tide 8:57 am
　　　　low 3:06 pm
nearing low
in the description of Joyce's
ocean one cloud as centerpiece
reaction
here piles of rock as
though bottom of the clay pot
awakening alms clinking
what of offered direction
being too shy
(to notice)
(to wander)
(to ask)
always in parentheses
the brief performance
of erasure

cantaloupe as in
revealed bearing

then did the city arrive

the skyscraper scaffolding
hanging just nearly back
among the earliest ingrained

memories the men whistling
mother then pregnant

the city in posturing
brings with it 3 things:
a cooler, beer, camera

ocean as background

from the crane,
wood in motion
        swinging cement
      with all of that
        hammer

abuelita says the sand
falls in pockets
from so much extraction

that she fell through
gentle footstep

in the reapplication
everything so
quickly planned—

fill in fortune
        cast aside
            part time/future retirement

staring at the metal instead of
    ocean

thumping heartbeat of wood
    hitting wave
        pounding again & again
        its way

to the benefit of the local Cemex operation
increased demand for building materials
known as Bayano

to secure contracts for projects
to supply all maintenance concrete
Canal/Metro line/Cinta/year on year double digit
the country now in the process of importing cement
Titan America/hydroelectric dam
flooded into
further demand/damned
name every company

special workshop on cement art in the labeled tropics
special delivery flashes across the screen in capital letters, yellow
rectangular backing, from the company most recently—

delay as in consideration of poor quality of cement early on
Argo wins Canal
for a price increase
reaching concrete milestone
a projected lifespan

to control the energy dissipation
aggregate stockpiles
of flake ice
the wing wall next to the ocean
3 million cubic meters

to speed up exports of _____ gas to _____
every company named

the Metro line as it snakes its way north
stockpile from the ground/in the ground/to the

To have a lack of aeration
as in negation transmitted
in absence of solitude
    solicitude of decomposition
if in some way alone
    or split apart

        out of

        to find
        out of

    how in knowing what
        we are not allowed

in the task of destruction
  after the visa acquired
enloca–ing

  quickly self allowing
       collapsure
    but incompletely
    ungenerously

  the hills also
     encircling

  like the claustrophobia
  of the room
  the man
  the country in accompaniment
  the line of hills
  with no clouds

  the roosters already
    marking insomnia

hanging
　　to dramatize
　　what is envisioned
　　cyclical collapsure
& fermented leavings/
　　returns
　　quite naturally/spoken of
　　change the hid down
　　now/branch/trunk between
buttcheek

to be enough less agile as
to
some approaching entity
shadow in sputtering sunlight
through which happenstance
or rooster crowing
the registers kept changing
& quickly moss
took back body

to walk together then
separate / this
as the car stalling out nearby
at first suspecting

in rock hard deposit
out-savoury-ing
at the hotel's banquet buffet

the social stratum crossed
again in passing

it was a fully built path
it looked like decades ago
but might have been last
year

the people who were doing
real work were
but some

—the old path that led to the tree seat
& the climbing vine led also
to the backyard of a
millionaire's house.
swans, peacocks, caged toucans,
& a squat-faced angry dog
a chandelier as large as
a person

an ushering out of / protected
from as in these (mostly)
empty well-manicured lots
that no one must walk thru

Beside the hammock in
which I write men
shoveling emptying &
transporting cement
with purpose as of yet unclear
possible storage
facility of maker
the old man owner
who stood before the eggs

if the road to the inside of
was built less than one hundred
years ago
the sounds if we are seated
on top of gurgling
only masked over by

———

some grey swatch of presence
the clouds over Gaital
this morning that will
make the last stretch of
the climb a challenge

over the chest neck &
head—
  the wind in the midst of journey

construction / quantities

been lifted from the notion of
breathless

yes, who cares, this is the
being (I) (we) create

you though understand the
future conditional

good day to each in
passing

buenas

     X

    cut short
hunger as an escaped entity
        foreign

the partition uncrumbling

& atone for falling fields

/
like a trellis
in climbing
the bad attitude surveillance
just as in

seed disturbances/dependencies

the open air in which
connected back to
     —questions of finance—

     one little step (at a time) (cemento)
sidewalk—o—rain—belligerent
     & what of licking

furnished by the cold/prolonged

how (has) (is) the archeological
     site as significant as claimed

how in walking past what
is desired to be looked at
is avoided
so that the honest curiosity
is saved for introspection

a study of people
a climate
a rationalized destruction

how were the burial (plots) (cities)
preserved for so long
& whenever they would be made
public how much would be
accounted for stolen
    —every time tangled
    basket of pyramid serpent haunting

by what you could not see
    but were told was there

questions compiled from various
how in terms of the plots of land
land ownership / eased grace
most efficient yields/
cost-productive / in terms of
the quality of / why does it
end here
becomes one piece cross-hatched
promised
red as in the clay-soil paintings
when your body has
been tricked into an outsider
status / hand as in the
burning sensations of
post cleaning acid
quizzed fortune been
returned
and is this/that how ma(n)y
feed/feet/meters above sea level

just long enough for
the metro now
the ride cost still
undetermined/to be in unexpected
understanding of uncertainty
that the line of crop
so abruptly end(ing)(s)—
"you like me so much
that I bring you" (music notes)
me gustas
capitán de amor/
pirata
the thick offshoot of the
horse's bones
quick as besos/baseless
    being
you feel a little thick now—

the strength of the new
as I causation/thigh/unreadable

this is the part of the project
when the break
(of illegibility)
(or the inquiry)
for for thou investigation

it has a soul that speaks
        to itself

        /
can I see the lines of land

there are places people
feel they are always
leaving
admité era uno de esos
para mí

        /

another & another befallings
the country you could not
recognize inside the country
you could—
    this would bring out your
    tragedies—singularly
    craven
back in the city who would
call for you

only naming in abstraction

the powerful ones naming in
concretized realities

to be helpful naming

the U.S. mindsway

not that everything was over before you knew it
    speak false captioning

COMPOSTA/COMPUESTO

A veces estoy más en un lugar que
others / it makes a difference where I
diferencia / muchos de los antiguos
of communities, both as in notions
nociones de vivir y lugar, un líder o guru
to guide / authoritatively instruct
si el diseño está supuesto a ser autoparticipatorio
participatory and an individual doubled
su participación real a cuál
degree of witnessing, how many
bromas en la panga o acompañamientos
if we mold things with our hands—
como podrían rápidas inst(i)(a)laciones o el
the kid size clay oven or the trapeze
pasado de repente o el bañarse entre una
among a 70 million year old entity
Debajo del árbol en el cual estoy
exploring/practicing/creating a ritual of
cierta manera de arraigamiento aunque en el aire
a mixture with green and brown materials—
un raíz especialmente elegante
stretches below my hand
cuando estoy boca abajo
by ankles I can nearly touch it and
a veces logro hacerlo—cambiando
whatever movement or creating it—
girar un poco más
The time we/here cannot be rapidly

diseccionado, aunque lo intentamos
it last night, as in the microscope
que funciona, pero con un pedazo
    piece slightly or fully broken
y aun caundo escribo esto, alguien
    approaching or distancing, footsteps
    sobre hojas, ramas
    and other decomposing
    descomponiendose
    to look at de-compositing
/composición como ~~lo má~~ creación
 without qualifiers

(END)NOTES

"Suelo" was written during Estudio Nuboso's January 2014 inter-disciplinary residency of the same name, held in Veraguas, Panamá, and co-facilitated by Ela Spalding, Claire Pentecost, Brian Holmes, and participants.

"On Suelo | Soil" was written at the end of January, in Coclé.

"Tide" was written beside the Pacific in Los Santos not far from where my mom was born and where some of the work I was then translating by Melanie Taylor Herrera takes place. Though there were periodic waves of medusas/jellyfish, days of watching, towards the end of February a particularly potent bloom came through.

"Cement" was written in March in Coclé, but also at times in Panamá (Province) along a beach cemented in memory. Later, the metro was inaugurated in Panamá (City) on April 4, 2014. I rode on it the first free day with my abuelita, George, and neighbors. Originally also scheduled for 2014, the third locks were opened June 26, 2016.

The text of "Composta/Compuesto" was created in 2015 for the dance videopoem "for Suelo Composta/Compuesto Soil." The materials in the video are from the Suelo residency. On the first day we gathered leaves, some brought in, if I remember correctly, in sweet-smelling bags from the nearest city, and we began to follow the recipe, pulling fibers from coconut husks and laying out organics collected and saved by residents. Quickly what had seemed dead became a living source. Though this text was originally written mostly in English, some of it was translated into Spanish by Carla Escoffery for Estudio Nuboso's SUELO booklet and I translated the rest. "Composta/Compuesto" is a splicing together of those texts. Language of inheritance and disinheritance. Alter(n)ation of lines, alter(n)ation of languages, resulting in reiteration, loss, and what may read like mistranslation. Neither a translation nor a bilingual flow. If one is bilingual (Spanish/English), one is (still) not getting the content of the original text. And if one knows only one of the languages, one is also making up a meaning, or believing in a sound or a seemingly rational growth. One is conjuring truth and life. There are missteps, naivetés, chops, and growth patterns to be in communication with.

The cover image is made from two photos layered together. One is from Cerro Ancón (a hill returned to Panamá after the 1977 Torrijos–Carter Treaties) looking onto Casco Antiguo (Panama City's second colonial settlement). At the base of the hill sits El Chorillo (a neighborhood bombed in 1989 during the U.S. invasion). The Cinta Costera 3 (a coastal highway inaugurated April 2014, opposed by residents and UNESCO) winds through the bay. The other photo was taken during the Suelo residency (of the ground, the circle of leaves, and the petals going dry).

ACKNOWLEDGMENTS

Thank you to the editors and curators of the installation *Big Splash*; the journals *Horse Less Review*, *LIT*, *New American Writing*, *a Perimeter*, *Under a Warm Green Linden*, *Tzak*, and *Word For/Word*; Estudio Nuboso's booklet *SUELO Vol. 1*; and the anthologies *The Wandering Song: Central American Writing in the United States* and *Best American Experimental Writing 2018*.

Friends, family, caretakers, neighbors, strangers, and acquaintances tended to, had patience with, and made this book possible. Thank you. Thank you Estudio Nuboso, Suelo, Festival San Francisco de la Montaña, public libraries, land, water, air, space, protectors of commons. Thank you Suelo participants: Anne, Anthony, Brian, Christ, Claire, Débora, Ela, Gertrudis, Héctor, Jennifer, Jorge, Juana, Kevin, Mariana, Mir, Olidis, Patrick, Paola, Pauline, Roman, Rose, Sylvie.

Deep gratitude to Ela Spalding's photo series *Entre suelo y concreto* and dance video series *Entre cielo y concreto*, Claire Pentecost's essay "Notes from the Underground" and *Soil-erg* project, and to the collective embroidery *Ofrenda al agua* begun by Pati Cepeda and cared for (in 2014) by Veronica Moreno. Thank you to Débora Rivera for sharing the compost recipe. Thank you Jennifer Spector for starting the day.

Amanda y momma and poppa and Page and Allan. George. Rosemary. Ariana, Travis. Thank you Kazim, Stephen, Lindsey, HR, Andrea, and all of Nightboat.

Thank you Asociación Centro de Estudios y Acción Social Panameño, Centro El Tucán, Los Rapaces, UA Poetry Center, UNO-Madrid summer 2007, Asociación de Mujeres María Auxiladora, Honeysuckle Tea House, Jaime & Equinox to Solstice, Oreba Chocolate, Mini, Caitlin, Inven, Erbey, Ivan, Emmanuel, Deida, Jorge, Farahni, Carlos, Rosita, Shaila, David, Madeline, Donald, Jackie, Hugo, Alafia, Julia, Kelly, Fadi, Mike, Josh, Charlie, Baz, Sarah, Matthew, Allie, Rainy, Jason, Erin, Chris, Lisa, Wendy, Renee, Gail, César, Patri, Maureen, Drew, Jamison, Nanette, Aja, Carie, Nicole, Katherine, Rebecca, Luigi, Francis, Kate, Antonio, Annie, Ani, Anny, Bienvenida, Edilberto, Jennifer, Alibel, Charlotte, Daniel, Celia, Dari, Gaby, Ada, Melanie, José Luis, Edgar, Markela, Natalie, Ytsel, Kerry, Brynna, reading rabbits, Nathan, Crystal, Jessica, Susanna, Gaurav, Jacob, Judith, Myung, Steve, Karen, Brenda, Aaron, Barbara, Noah, Kevin, Robin, Petra, Stephanie, Brandy, Toni, Jo, Galia, Stanzi, Courtney, Nancy, Jane, Boyer, Barbara, Laynie, Bill, Nancy, Amaud, Roberta, Chicu, Eric, Frank, Willy, Gladys, Francisco, thank you students, teachers. Thank you Maria, Ben, Shengyu, Justin, Grandma Elsie, Grandma Westhoff, Dana, Amanda, Inga, Amy, Don, my cousins, aunts, uncles, extended families, and friends. To the unnamed. And in other planes, Grandpa, Abuelito, Trish. You are also here in this space.

Geo, gracias por acompañarme.

CHRISTINA VEGA-WESTHOFF is a poet, translator, aerialist, and teaching artist. She lives in Buffalo, New York.

NIGHTBOAT BOOKS

Nightboat Books, a nonprofit organization, seeks to develop audiences for writers whose work resists convention and transcends boundaries. We publish books rich with poignancy, intelligence, and risk. Please visit our website, www.nightboat.org, to learn about our titles and how you can support our future publications.

The following individuals have supported the publication of this book. We thank them for their generosity and commitment to the mission of Nightboat Books:

Elizabeth Motika
Benjamin Taylor

In addition, this book has been made possible, in part, by grants from the National Endowment for the Arts and the New York State Council on the Arts Literature Program.